NEGATIVE
CRITICISM

NEGATIVE CRITICISM

**Its swath of destruction
and what to do
about it.**

SIDNEY B. SIMON

Cover Design by Gene Tarpey
Illustrations by Collin Fry

FIRST EDITION
©Copyright 1978 by Sidney B. Simon
All rights reserved. No portion of this book may be reproduced,
stored in a retrieval system, or transmitted in any form by any
means—electronic, mechanical, photocopying, recording, or
otherwise—without prior permission of the copyright owner.

Printed in the United States of America.

International Standard Book Number 1880424-07
Library of Congress Number 78-73334

9 8 7 6 5 4 3

This book is dedicated to Louis E. Raths, who died May 26, 1978. He was my teacher, my advisor, my colleague and my friend. His place in my life and my work has made all the difference. I will be eternally grateful to him.

Sidney B. Simon

CONTENTS

CHAPTER 1

THE KNIVES OF CRITICISM

It is a little after midnight. You have just come out of the last show at the movie. To save a block you cut through a dark alley. Halfway through it—just when you are beginning to relax—two men step out of the shadows. You hear a nasty metallic snick and suddenly there is the glint of knife blades in the feeble light.

What would you do?

I know what I would do.

Quickly I'd turn and throw a fearful look back up the alley. It is clear and free. A surge of adrenalin sends the blood pumping to my legs. Getting out of that alley I set a new indoor Olympic sprint record. The jogger in me has never seen such speed. Nothing seems sweeter than the glare of street lights and the chatter of people making their way to their cars. I look for a police officer and tell my story.

That is what everybody would do in such a situation, right?

But let me play you another version. The scene is the same. The two hulking men are coming at you with knives. But you keep strolling casually on to meet them. You throw up your arms and say, "I'm all yours. Let me feel the steel. I know it will help me in the long run."

They oblige by savagely thrusting the knives deep into your defenseless belly. You fall to the pavement writhing with pain. The men stand over you. You roll onto your stomach and gasp, "You'd better give me a couple in the back, too."*

Ridiculous?

Of course, but it is exactly what thousands upon thousands of us do each and every day by failing to recognize that the knives of negative criticism which people stick in us are just as sharp and deadly as those made of steel and borne by assassins.

Why?

Because our society has somehow conditioned us to accept the notion that criticism of all sorts is bound to be good for us. That it will make us more mature. That one of the marks of being a grown-up woman or man is the ability to absorb all sorts of critical jabs, barbs, and thrusts. That the more it hurts the better it is for us.

It is the purpose of this book to demonstrate that not only is this notion completely false, but in fact just the opposite is true—that the

---

*The author wishes to thank Sidney Cutbill, an as yet unsung poet of the human psyche, for coming up with this image.

"It's good for me."

unquestioning acceptance of negative criticism is one of the most destructive things we tolerate among the psychological hazards of life.

It is my conviction that most of us who would run for our lives when threatened with cold steel are programmed to stand and absorb any amount of negative criticism. There is something about it which freezes our normal mechanisms of self-preservation and escape. To the person who is wielding the knife of criticism—regardless of who he or she is, however ignorant, unfair, or unjust the remark—we say, in effect, "Please tell me more: I'm sure you are absolutely right and that I can learn and grow better from any old thing you have to say about me."

In other words, "Stab me. Push it in deep and twist if you like."

CHAPTER 2

THE HONESTY PIT

Do you mean that there is no value whatsoever in giving or receiving criticism? That we are supposed to go through life without learning from mistakes that should be recognized and pointed out to us? That we should not expect any reprimands, even when we are wrong or foolish or selfish or do anything else that people don't like?

For the moment I want to avoid a direct answer to those questions and say my point simply is that all criticism hurts. There is plenty of it for everybody. But the needless, heedless acceptance of negative criticism, especially in the early years of life, does as much permanent psychological damage to our lives as if we had been set upon by a hundred muggers with knives or guns.

And even knowing this, we do nothing to resist, escape, or fight back.

The reason, or at least a good part of the explanation for such strange behavior, lies, I'm convinced, in our social conditioning. We are living in a society—especially those of us involved in the human potential movement— which has set a high premium on honesty. It is the great sign, the banner which is to be the guiding principle of our actions and relationships with others. Above all we want to be honest— known as honest. The greatest compliment we can pay is to say of another, "He is an honest person."

But the word honesty has been so overused, it has lost a good part of its meaning. Like any banner that is waved continually, it has become tattered and worn. I am leery of people who use the word honesty in every other sentence. To me it has become a sort of hunting license issued to people who want to inflict negative criticism. When someone comes up to me and says, "I want to be perfectly honest with you . . . ," I brace myself. I know I'm not going to get a nice big bundle of praise, or even something soothingly neutral. What I can count on is a direct jab from the critical knife. All over the country, one-to-one and in group sessions, people are socking it to each other as often and as hard as they can—all under the great and noble banner of honesty.

What I want to stress in this book is not that honesty is bad, but that it needs to be clearly understood and applied. Honesty needs to be extended to its full range. To be honest with and about people is not simply to harp on their faults and mistakes. That is only one end of the scale of honesty, or only part of what it means to be honest. To limit it to the negative is the same as thinking you are getting full use of a piano when you play only the black keys.

The Honesty Pit

The full scale of truth must also include honest validation of people, honest affirmations of love, and honest appraisal of the vulnerability, frailty, and humanity of both ourselves and others.

To limit our understanding and uses of honesty only to the critical is much like trying to form a complete picture of human life by merely reading the daily newspaper and listening to the six o'clock news. Ninety percent of what we read and hear concerns the sensational, the controversial, the violent, the tragic, or the abnormal.

We would have a terribly narrow, frightening, and distorted picture of life if we limited our understanding of its richness and complexity to what we learn from the media. And we have an equally narrow and distorted view of human relationships if we limit our understanding of honesty to searching out, pointing to, and telling each other only the faults, mistakes, and disagreeable traits we observe—all in the name of honesty.

To do so is to fall into the dark, confining, ultimately destructive place I call the honesty pit.

CHAPTER 3

THE GOSSAMER THREAD

I have always found it helpful to imagine that between myself and every person with whom I have established some sort of relationship, there exists a gossamer thread. It is a beautiful, glistening, irridescent, fragile thread and a very precious connection between us. Whether it is the special relationship which I as a father have with my children, or the relationship which exists between me and each of my friends, or between myself and my students and colleagues—I see each as a separate, beautiful, fragile gossamer thread.

Imagine an individual gossamer thread connecting *you* to each person with whom *you* have some sort of relationship. Each thread is beautiful but *fragile*—I want to emphasize that word fragile.

Now there are various sorts of relationships. Obviously some are very casual. The thread exists all right, but it is not always being tested. Other relationships are much more important and vital in our lives, ones that are being stretched and pulled and strained and tested and polished every day. And the most significant of all of these are our vital love relationships.

18

"I think our gossamer thread
is getting a bit frayed."

What happens in a love relationship at the very beginning is that the two persons who are connected look down the length of the brand new gossamer thread and see nothing but glowing perfection. Take the case of a mother with her newborn baby. She sees nothing but flawless beauty in the object of her love. But what seems inevitably to happen in a love relationship is that one day (and it is never clear just why or how it starts) one of the parties looks down the thread and sees a speck, a flaw, something disturbing, something to disapprove of or be disappointed with. Immediately, under the banner of honesty, falsely convinced that pointing out the flaw is just bound to help the other and automatically restore perfection, they send a shock of criticism down the gossamer thread.

It may be a shock of general criticism: "Your color combinations are getting worse every day. Don't you care? Why would you wear that tie with that shirt?" Or: "You never stop eating, do you?" Or: "You're becoming more selfish every day."

Whatever it is, the shock goes speeding down the gossamer thread and into the consciousness of the other person. But it doesn't just sting a second and go away. It burns and tears away a chunk of the person, and to some degree a portion of the relationship is damaged.

If that sounds overly dramatic just stop and think for a moment. I defy anyone reading this book to tell me that she or he has ever felt indifferent, let alone uplifted, enriched, cheered up, or enhanced when put on the receiving end of a blast of criticism.

On the contrary, it is the opposite feeling which is experienced. Many of us feel physical discomfort. It may be your stomach which gives a sour roll, your heart may skip a beat, your mouth and throat go dry, your eyes grow narrow and tight and perhaps even squeeze out a bitter tear of anger or hurt. But I am still looking for the person who claims that criticism gives them a good, glowing feeling all over.

Perhaps we shouldn't be, but we are definitely diminished in some degree when criticized. And that feeling of diminishment is represented by the chunk of us that gets burned away by the shock of negative criticism.

I think that your own experience will confirm this almost universal reaction and feeling of diminishment. But, what is less well-recognized is that the shock of criticism also burns away a chunk of the person who *sends* it. The force or energy required to deliver the shock almost always diminishes the criticizer, too—just as surely as the battery which powers some rural electric fence gets depleted each time it shocks some hapless animal that runs against it.

This always happens, but it is easier to perceive in a love relationship where one really cares deeply for the person on the other end of the gossamer thread. Think back to the times when you've sparked off a criticism to someone you love—perhaps in sudden anger, or as a little revenge shot for some real or imagined slight.

Did you really feel better for doing it? Even as the surge is passing don't you generally regret having said what you did? If you are honest, you will admit that you feel somehow smaller—certainly you don't feel uplifted, enriched, enlarged, or joyful.

I can hear a reader protesting, "But why do we always have to feel enhanced, enriched, and joyful?"

Clearly, we don't. But I cannot find justification for feeling down, depressed, wounded, and withered.

From somewhere comes the myth that if we suffer, we will be better people. I don't believe that. I feel the human being was meant to be sunny, giving, caring, thoughtful, delighted, and delightful—and a whole string of other positive things. It is only as we get hurt, wounded, scarred and distressed that we become less than those positive things. Consequently, in our child-rearing, in our teaching, in our living, we need to do everything possible to reach back to the way we were meant to be—enriched, enhanced, and joyful.

We don't know why it happens this way, but it does. Perhaps if we were all big and strong and ruthlessly unfeeling—a bunch of Godzilla monsters—it would not be that way. But then we are not monsters, not machines. Machines don't feel, they just perform. The price of feeling, loving, and interacting with others may just be this brittleness, this sensitivity, this fragility in our relationships.

Getting back to the image of the gossamer thread, consider now that one shock has a way of triggering more. Like eating peanuts, it's impossible to stop with one. The rule of three seems to govern. Give one well-placed blast to knock the person down and send a couple more to keep them wallowing. Listen to how often we add, ". . . and furthermore," or, ". . . in addition, . . ."

But the receiving party doesn't stay down for long. They come right back with a counter-attack of their own: "You've said a lot about me, now let me tell you a few things about yourself."

And it's your turn to go down for awhile. The process can go on and on like some cartoon boxing match. A truce may be established, a limited peace. Then a day, or a week, or a month later it starts up again. But, as I said before, the shocks do not just pass harmlessly away. Sometimes I feel they are as dangerous as arsenic. The effect is cumulative. Old wounds open up, scar tissue is formed. More and more chunks have been burned away from both parties in the relationship, and remember, not just one chunk but two get destroyed from each criticism—one in the sender and one in the receiver.

When this goes on for a period of time what happens? When you look down the gossamer

"... run over by negative criticism."

thread, you no longer see anything near perfection. What you see now is someone scarred and diminished—far from the object of perfect beauty you saw initially. And when the other person looks back up the thread from their perspective they see the same thing. Both begin to wonder what they saw in each other in the first place.

So the gossamer thread, which has grown less lustrous and more fragile from carrying all that destructive voltage, begins to get a real overload. With less and less regard for the relationship on both sides, the criticisms fly back and forth like lightning. The thread begins to hum with heavier and heavier putdowns and insults, the really killing cruelty. The thread cannot take this kind of heavy voltage—it was never designed to. As the escalation mounts, the voltage increases, and the gossamer thread snaps and tears apart. So do the people.

When the threads of a love relationship are severed in this way, what you get is divorce, a runaway child, brothers and sisters who refuse to speak to each other for the rest of their lives. When the threads of more casual relationships are broken, we see the creation of estrangement, enmity, jealousy, revenge, cruelty—you name it.

Yet we all know people who have managed to keep the gossamer thread connecting their relationship intact for years—for a lifetime. Was their relationship somehow less fragile than others? Is it because they are truly perfect people? Or, have they somehow managed to protect and insulate their thread—wrap or coat it in such a way that it is as strong as a steel cable—a bond so strong that hacksaws or welding torches cannot cut through it?

The answer to the last question is, yes, and a major purpose of this book is to try and discover how to make steel cables out of your own gossamer threads.

CHAPTER 4

THE RED
PENCIL
MENTALITY

Traditionally, editors use red pencils to mark
mistakes and corrections on galley proofs of
type that have been set for newspapers, books,
and magazines. Teachers use red pencils, too.
Remember when the term paper you worked on
so hard and long came fluttering back onto your
desk practically covered with bold red lines
pointing out errors of fact and spelling? Can you
remember how destroyed you felt? Almost like
your pride and joy had been taken out and
machine-gunned—as if each one of those awful
red marks was a hole in your skin?

Well, there is a whole critical approach to life
that I like to call "the red pencil mentality." It is
an attitude that searches out errors and marks
them out boldly for everyone to see.

The red pencil people, operating under the
banner of honesty-at-all-costs, put a lot of strain
on all the gossamer threads of the relationships
they are in. They feel compelled to use their
red pencils on those they love for the sake of
improving and perfecting them. What they are
really doing is sharpening the knives of negative
criticism so that they can cut an ever wider
swath of destruction in human self-esteem.

There's a red pencil clipped into nearly everybody's psychological pocket, but perhaps they are most readily observed in the hands of parents. I love to ask mothers and fathers to take a piece of paper, draw a vertical line down its middle and then think back to the last dozen or so things they can recall saying to their children—last night at the dinner table, while watching television in the evening, as everyone is getting ready for bed, in the morning before breakfast, as the kids leave for school.

On the left side of the line I tell them to list all the corrections and suggestions for improvement they made and on the right side I ask them to list all the positive things— affirmations, validations, compliments, expressions of love or regard.

The left side quickly gets filled with such comments as:

"Get those elbows off the table."

"Cut your meat in smaller pieces and use your knife, not your fork."

"Don't talk with food in your mouth."

"Get your hair out of your eyes; if you'd get it cut, that wouldn't happen."

"Did you put your underwear in the hamper?"

"You've got on too much eye shadow; take some of it off."

"Do you really think that blue gunk does anything for you?"

"Your room looks like a pigsty."

27

The Red Pencil Mentality

"Stand up straight; take your hands out of your pockets."

"You'll never learn algebra watching television."

"That's the sixth phone call tonight."

"If you don't put that bike away, it will be stolen and I'm not buying another one."

"Can't you ever wear anything but those ragged jeans?"

"Why do you want to disgrace us?"

But on the right side you seldom get much of anything except, "Goodnight" or "Pleasant dreams."

The huge imbalance between the lists is a dramatic yet dreary demonstration of just how much of what parents tell their children boils down to criticism of one sort or another. It may not seem so completely destructive taken one item at a time—neither does one cigarette. But added together it is graphic proof of just how pervasive and destructive the red pencil mentality is.

And, while it may be that in their role as parents, men and women use their red pencils most actively, they are using them in many other relationships as well. You don't have to be a parent to benefit from the paper exercise. Just make a list of how often your own mother and father have red-penciled you, or how often you have used yours to mark out unsatisfactory items on a friend's or fellow-worker's appearance, behavior, habits, or performance.

The red pencil mentality is highly contagious. We all seem to catch the habit of looking for the flaw, the mistake, the awkward and the ugly in others. Perhaps it is the flip side of the Golden Rule—"Do unto others before they do unto you." All I know is that there is an awful lot of it going around.

On the other hand, people who have known their share of affirmations, approval, and admiration, literally walk taller, laugh more abundantly and obviously love more fearlessly.

One of the things to notice about people who have lived in a heavy red pencil family situation (or other relationship), is that they seldom feel good about themselves. They have lived with and absorbed a staggering number of putdowns. Their self-esteem is so low you couldn't slide a playing card under it. They are quick—almost anxious—to set themselves up for the rejection they feel is bound to come.

A difficult issue is the one that arises from people on one side saying, "Learning isn't meant to be easy or soft or gentle. People grow from and through pain and discomfort. To protect people from such realities would be to do them a genuine disservice." The other side argues for gentleness and patience and softening of the blows of the learning process. My own observations and experience cause me to come firmly on the latter side. But that doesn't mean that the issue is resolved for everyone.

We go looking . . .

CHAPTER 5

SIX DELICIOUS FLAVORS OF VULTURE FOOD

It is no wonder, then, that all of us are afflicted to some degree by one insidious outcome of negative criticism—the self-putdown. We've been so deeply immersed in the red pencil mentality for most of our lives that we practice it on ourselves as an unnatural exercise in doom and gloom.

If I criticize myself loud enough and often enough, maybe I'll improve. At any rate, maybe criticism won't hurt quite so much coming from myself. More likely, it grows like a tick, feeding on distress and fear. And, like all forms of negative criticism, it amounts only to sharpening the knives of negative criticism to cut a swath of destruction—in this case, self-destruction.

In an earlier book* I visualized self-putdowns as food for the psychological vultures which hover around people day and night. Every self-putdown is a meal for these scary and ugly birds with their cruel beaks and sharp talons. The meal consists of a piece of our own self-image. In that book we went through a day in the life of a teenage girl, dramatizing the

*VULTURE: *A Modern Allegory on the Art of Putting Oneself Down* Argus #20984, $2.25)

many wonderous ways she found to fatten her vultures.

But self-putdowns (vulture food) come in six different flavors: Intelligence (IQ); Social; Family; Creativity; Sexual; and Physical.

INTELLIGENCE (IQ)

It may come as a surprise, since few people are willing to talk about their feelings of inadequacy with others, but virtually everyone feels that he or she is not as smart as they ought to be—or as they would like to be. Some are conscious of particular lapses or gaps in their ability to think, remember, calculate, and the like. They work hard at avoiding situations where this particular weakness might show them up. But there are many who feel inadequate at almost every level of mental effort. Such people go through the day telling themselves that they are stupid, moronic, incompetent.

This is prime vulture food, and like most self-putdowns, a poor mental self-image produces a vicious circle. The person who goes off to the grocery having just written down everything she wanted to buy so she wouldn't forget anything promptly forgets to bring the list itself. She calls herself stupid for this and goes into a mental freeze which blocks her ability to remember much of what was on the list. Which, in turn, convinces her that she is indeed a true superstar among memory idiots. This sort of freeze-panic-putdown cycle carries over into schoolwork and then, in later years, to the job.

The Party

Many people suffer a sort of cumulative fear of thinking which makes them shrink from opportunities and challenges which they could really handle quite readily if they were only able to have a balanced appraisal of their own powers. It is a frightening and crippling putdown which afflicts more people than we realize.

SOCIAL

People are said to be social animals, but very few of us really feel adequate in social gatherings such as parties. Many of us doubt our ability to carry on intelligent, much less brilliant, conversations; we feel certain that after a few minutes our lack of knowledge, depth and sophistication will be unmasked and no one will want to talk to us and stay with us for very long.

If you have ever wondered why so much alcohol is consumed at parties, it is because so few people feel good enough about their social abilities to carry on without its blurring support. If one were able, somehow, to see the number of vultures which come in through the door with all the party guests, you'd run for your life.

The socially inadequate person finds endless ways of feeding his or her vultures. Anything can serve: so simple a thing as coming into someone else's house at Christmas, seeing a table covered with Christmas cards and comparing that big display with the handful he or she has received. (You *know* you've got a vulture when you begin to question if all of them are this year's cards.) Others put themselves down when they

Six Flavors

learn of a party to which they have not been invited—even when they scarcely know the hosts and would not really care to go in the first place. But not getting the invitation brings out the vultures in squadrons.

FAMILY

Perhaps because they endure for so long (or have to be endured), or because they are so complex, family relationships are one of the most abundant sources of vulture food. Here, expectations of self have no visible ceilings. It is very difficult, for instance, to find a mother who feels she is really doing her job well. I defy you to interview forty mothers and find one who will say with confidence that she is doing a fine job as mother to her family. Even if she feels she is doing a splendid job for six days in a row, should she lose her temper and yell at her children on the seventh, she immediately labels herself as "that kind of screaming mother—the sort I really am down deep."

For her vulture never sleeps, you see; it is always there flapping about above her head, waiting for the chance to tear off a piece of her self-esteem. For the record, most fathers feel even worse about their over-all performance.

In the same way, few people really feel totally adequate in their roles as sons or daughters, grandparents, grandsons or granddaughters. To a somewhat lesser extent, this can extend to roles as aunts, uncles, nephews, nieces— even cousins.

Did you know that many recovering alcoholics go off the wagon at Christmas, and that there are more suicides then, and that school and family counselors experience their peak work loads at that time? It is true. There is something about family relationships at Christmas which trigger all those grotesque feelings of inadequacy so many people have in their family roles.

Christmas is a grand time for vultures. So are Father's Day and Mother's Day and most anniversaries. Want to find your own vulture? Just ask yourself, "Did I do enough last year for the birthday of the person I love most?"

CREATIVITY

The assurance with which most people proclaim their lack of creativity is truly amazing. It is painful—but so common as to be almost boring—to hear people say in countless ways and about so many things: "I'm just not very creative." Try complimenting someone on how they've decorated their apartment or home.

"Oh, it's all right, I guess, but I'm just not very creative that way."

Or thank someone for a special handmade gift at Christmas which you really appreciated for the beauty and time it represents.

"Oh, it's nothing, really—I mostly followed the directions in a book, you know."

The instant self-putdown of virtually everything related to creativity is nearly universal. Perhaps because it is something which

Christmas

most people confer high status to, or because there are relatively few objective standards for establishing what is creative. It is associated in most minds with something which thousands applaud simultaneously, or which is recognized by proclamations in the media or by awards.

When I say that the creativity self-putdown afflicts almost everyone, I think of the author, Ernest Hemingway. Even after he was awarded the ultimate accolade, the Nobel Prize for Literature, he worried about the failure of his "creative juices" and could be set to brooding by the slightest criticism from far lesser writers.

Creativity vultures have no doubts whatsoever about their own ability to create— to create great gaping holes in a self-image.

SEXUALITY

People carry tremendous feelings of inadequacy about sexuality. Again, it is something far more common than most realize because it lies in an area which few feel free to discuss without acute embarrassment. But counselors will tell you that the most ravishingly beautiful women and the most handsome and virile men are seldom totally free of self-doubts about their sexuality.

The subject is complex and too involved to explore fully here, but we do know that in the sexual area, people are highly influenced by what they read and hear. Sexuality is perniciously pervasive in books, films, and other media. Everyone listens, watches, and secretly compares. The cult of mutual orgasm has raised the end of the rainbow to sacred desirability. Those who fail to achieve this physiological Nirvana feel immediately hopeless about their performance. (One of my students once joked, with great precision, about the fact that the reasons for leaks in all those water beds rose not from the action in the bed but from the beaks of all the vultures that were diving and striking during lovemaking.)

Suffice it to say that a lot of trouble arises through invidious comparisons. Most men and women are able to sit and watch O. J. Simpson, Walter Payton or Chris Evert perform incredible feats on a playing field or tennis court without putting themselves down. They have the good sense to know that there's no possible way they could ever perform like one of these exceptional professional athletes. Ah, but let one whisper of some sexual attribute or performance that they have not managed come to their ears and they immediately assume themselves inadequate—and the vultures dive and tear.

PHYSICAL

This last broad category of negative self-criticism is perhaps the most troublesome of all for many people because we cannot hide our physical selves as easily as we can cover up our feelings of social or sexual inadequacies. (Cover them, yes, but escape from them, no.)

There are very few people who get up in the morning, run to the mirror and say, "Oh, what a

*"Beneath this patina of quivering
self-doubt breathes a beautiful,
creative human being."*

beautiful person I am." Products as we are of the pervasive red pencil mentality, we immediately see all the bad features—the pimples, wrinkles, and sags—that cause the putdowns that feed the particularly vicious vultures that make their base in the bathroom.

Comparisons are continually at work here, too. There is always somebody who is prettier, more buxom, more slender, stronger, more graceful, with a better complexion, with bigger eyes, a flatter stomach, a better nose or more lustrous hair. It is little consolation to most of us, busy feeding the mirror vultures every morning, that Hollywood bathrooms are full of stars and starlets doing exactly the same thing.

Having explored the six flavors of vulture food and seen what wonderfully fertile sources of self-putdowns they provide, it may be a good time to point to the main idea about the whole vulture image: *No baby has a vulture lurking over its crib.*

There is not a single toddler stumbling about the family room who feels the least bit inadequate about her or his intelligence, social graces, family relationships, physical appearance, creativity, or sexuality. Babies are marvelously whole and adequate little creatures. They have no doubts about their perfection and every person near them confirms their own good opinion of themselves.

Which makes the logic inescapable: every single vulture which people have circling about them has been created by something or someone else. *What creates vultures is negative criticism and what feeds them are the resulting self-putdowns we inflict on ourselves every day—self-putdowns that have been internalized out of negative criticism.*

Somewhere, sometime, somebody stuck the muggers' knives of negative criticism into you— and you accepted the blades. These wounds have attracted the vultures of self-putdowns that feed on ever larger chunks of your weakened self-esteem.

Once upon a time someone stuck you with the knifelike comment: "If you weren't so selfish, always thinking about yourself first, you would do more for the family." And your first "family" vulture was born.

The day you proudly brought home a test paper graded 86 percent, and somebody said, "That's a long way from 100 percent—can't you do better?"—that's when your first IQ vulture was hatched.

The time you overheard someone whisper, "Jane would be a nice-looking little girl if only she weren't quite so skinny"—and you created the first of many physical appearance vultures ready for flight training.

The men and women who work on Madison Avenue in Manhattan and in advertising agencies throughout the country—and the world—know all about negative criticism and vultures. In fact they consider them so real and so universal that they spend millions of dollars each year to tell us about products designed to appeal to people already personally convinced of their inadequacies. Thus, the creams and salves for acne and pimples, all sorts of hair curlers and straighteners, padded bras and muscle-builders, sex manuals and devices, elevator shoes and eye shadow, books to improve your memory, pills to make you thin and pills to make you gain weight. The list could go on and on.

Negative criticism comes from virtually every area of life. Clearly it comes from parents and grandparents. It comes from teachers, "friends," neighbors, acquaintances, and the people we work with. But it is coming at us in a steady stream through the media, as well. Even though we should know enough to be conscious that the message is not directed at us personally, the ad people know that we are so insecure, so plagued by the same sorts of vultures, that we will indeed take it personally enough to run right out and buy their products.

To sit through a typical evening of television commercials is to be made to feel unattractive, overweight, too old, full of gas, afflicted with headaches—generally a total mess. The media count on us feeling this way, not only to sell the products which offer promise of direct and almost magical solution for our particular affliction, but to sell other products—including cars, cameras, recordings—that we buy in order to make us forget how bad we feel about ourselves.

If you've ever doubted that vultures are real, ask yourself why manufacturers are willing to spend millions for just a few seconds of television's prime time—prime time for preying on the greatest national pastime of them all, putting ourselves down.

CHAPTER 6

GET OFF
MY FOOT!

Now we come to the crossroads of this book.
We have talked about the harm that negative
criticism is capable of doing. We have, at least by
indirection, made it clear that people who
just stand there and take it, or worse, actively
accept it and walk toward the knives of negative
criticism, are their own worst enemies. We have
talked about the swath of destruction resulting
from accepting negative criticism blindly
and then using it to feed the vulture with
self-putdowns.

But criticism is never a one-way street, as we
saw in the chapter on the gossamer thread.
We need to make some important distinctions.
It would be an ideal world in which everyone
respected the feelings, rights, and sensitivities
of everyone else. In such a world no criticism
need be given and none received. But in reality
people are walking all over each other every day.
And nowhere in this book do I mean to advocate
that anyone should serve as a doormat out of
some idealized conviction that it is far better to
accept any and all sorts of pain or humiliation
because speaking out might hurt or offend the
tender psyche of the one who is trampling
on you.

Not at all.

The person who just stands there like a sheep in the aisle of a crowded bus while someone grinds a foot into their instep and takes the pain while saying nothing—and worse, not even moving the foot in case it might upset the grinder—is absurd. It hurts. The other person, whether conscious or not of what he is doing, has no right to inflict this sort of pain. It doesn't matter what sort of relationship he may have with you, or his mother, or whether he even knows you or not. *Tell him to get the bleep off your foot.*

There are hundreds of more subtle but highly comparable situations in life. Generally they have to do with "public" places. The person who takes your parking place, the road hog, the lady who jumps ahead of you in line, the man who is blowing cigar smoke on everyone in the elevator, the person whose umbrella is dripping down your neck as you wait for the light to change— all of these people are standing on your foot. They are doing something thoughtless; they are infringing on your rights; they are causing you some form of pain.

Tell them to knock it off, desist, depart— STOP! That isn't criticism. And it seldom hurts their feelings because they were merely unaware. On the other hand, they might just be rude and insensitive. In either case, it is not apt to cause them permanent damage to be told, "Get off my foot!

"Would you please desist?"

Let us suppose that the tables are turned.
That it is you who are the offending party.
You may say to yourself, on hearing the
obviously justified protest of the person on
whose foot you just stepped, "I did something
stupid." Well, you did. But you know that it
was an accident, or that you were completely
distracted. It is the sort of perfectly obvious and
justified fact that you should be able to handle
without letting it infect you with a self-putdown
virus. (There are exceptions, of course, if you
are already afflicted with the "I'm-really-a-
clumsy-lout" sort of vulture.)

So far we have been talking about more or
less random encounters between strangers.
There are, however, many times when people
with whom you have far closer and more lasting
relationships step on your foot in one way or
another. And here you are faced with a more
delicate and difficult problem.

On the one hand, you don't want to be—
should never be—a doormat. On the other,
these are people you care about and who care
about you. If it is a one-time thing—someone
is literally standing on your foot or slamming
a car door on your hand—there is really no
problem. You say, "Stop it!" "Get off!" or
"Will you please look at what you are doing?"
The offending party feels upset for a few minutes
and probably sorry, but unless he or she did it
on purpose, there is really no negative criticism
to be stored away.

But close relationships have a way of presenting us with many varieties of more chronic sorts of foot-stomping. The husband who never quite remembers to call home when he is going to be late is standing on the foot of the wife who is watching her carefully prepared dinner dry up to a ghastly scorch on the bottom of the pan; the wife who can never quite be ready on time to go out is doing the same to a husband who prides himself on being punctual. The friend who is always borrowing a dollar or two and never remembers to pay it back is a chronic foot-treader. So is the son who never remembers to turn off the basement light and the daughter who always misses the clothes hamper with her dirty unmentionables. Let us not even honor the phantom who squeezes the toothpaste tube at the top and never puts the cap back on with a mention. And, I'd be willing to wager there is not a father alive who has not felt the whole family grinding away on his ingrown toenail when he starts trying to round up all the tools that are missing from their appointed places when he starts to fix something.

Just to take up the last item: this tool-chase has occurred not just once or twice, but virtually every Saturday morning back into the dim mists of time so far as the father is concerned. He has spoken about it politely, nicely; he has spoken about it firmly. Now he is simply quite mad as hell and he yells at the first available potential offender: "Can't you stupid kids remember, just once, to put my tools back where you got them from? I could have trained a pet rock to remember better than you do."

Here we certainly have an expression of "Get off my foot!" But we've also got a long sharp knife of negative criticism coming on as well.

It is the same with another parent who finds the usual sodden, sour, mildewing towel and washcloth festering in the middle of the bathroom hamper when collecting the weekly laundry. The parent is going to unload accumulated frustrations on the first possible culprit seen—guilty or not. But chances are, unless the parent stops and thinks for a moment, he or she is going to breed a future vulture.

What should the parents do? Be doormats? Swallow hard and smile—grin and bear it one more time?

Definitely not. But at the same time they must realize that these are more or less timeless problems—classics, cliches even—of family life. When they were children, they did such things and their children are now continuing the cycle. There is no easy, new, wonder-drug cure for these classic foot-stompings of family life. But Thomas Gordon of the Parent Effectiveness Training (PET) program suggests three highly useful steps for what he calls an "I-Message," which a parent (or anyone involved in a chronic interpersonal foot-stomping situation) can use to good effect. Rather than simply explode, throwing the knives of negative criticism in all directions in a deadly hail that does nothing to solve the basic problem, Gordon suggests a three-part approach:

1. Say clearly how you feel when . . .
2. Describe the offensive behavior in a nonblameful way.
3. Explain the reason for your feeling, or the consequences or results of the behavior.

Let's take the case of a youthful driver who makes a habit of parking the family car half on the drive and half on the lawn. He has been told about this several times. It will not do much good simply to blow up and say, "I've really had it up to here with you about tearing up the yard." That's a rough way of covering Steps 1 and 2, but you have to be less blameful if you really want to get through. You have to add the third part—stress the consequences.

Say, perhaps: "I see you've run the car off the drive again. You know that this really upsets us. You know that your father and I take pride in the lawn and we would rather use the money and time it takes to repair it to do something good for the family."

An important fourth step is not simply to say this and walk away in a huff (to dump and run), but to stay with it, inviting and expecting a response. If there is an explanation, listen to it. If there is nothing more than a counter-blast, hear it out. Listen, care, repeat if necessary, but get closer to really solving the problem. Gordon

". . . 1. I am irate . . . 2. It is a filthy mess . . .
3. If it happens again
I'll have to call a meeting
of the negotiating committee!"

says that after you deliver your "I-Message," you stay around and actively listen—lots.

And sometimes, with those we love or care for, this may involve a certain amount of negotiation—something like a labor and management contract dispute.

Negotiators do not give up their claim or position. They are simply willing to hear what the other side has to say and what it wants. History has proved that negotiation is better than fighting—better than continuing destructive warfare. It works this way in personal relationships as well. Following the three steps of Gordon and then listening to the other side at least gets the problem out in the open. Both sides are aware of the other's feelings. The side with less of a leg to stand on may realize that they could or should change their behavior. The other side may get some glimpse of at least part of the reason for the behavior. Perhaps a compromise or exchange can be worked out—a new behavioral contract issued.

One mother I know proved to be a brilliant negotiator. Plagued by two children—and a husband—who dropped their dirty clothes wherever they happened to take them off, she had been blowing her top at all of them indiscriminately. Even when one or two of them would remember and deposit clothes in the bathroom hamper, one would forget, and the mother would dump and run on all of them— or the first one who happened to cross her charging path.

The situation, trivial as it sounds, got very tender. Nobody likes to be blamed for something he didn't do. But as far as the mother was concerned, the whole family—or at least one of them—was always standing on her foot.

She finally decided she would issue a new contract. She announced to them all that whenever she found dirty clothes outside the hamper she would go ahead and pick them up (she was having to do this anyway) and say not a word. But the person they belonged to owed her a three-minute backrub, collectable whenever she wanted it, and done lovingly.

That way, she figured, she couldn't lose—and she didn't. She got quite a number of excellent backrubs which her children and husband learned to deliver with tender devotion. The whole family became more aware of each other as people, and, best of all, the air was clear and freed of one heck of a lot of negative criticism. (And, I personally feel that there will be a lot more character and feeling built into a child who learns how to give a good backrub than in one who learns how to put dirty underwear into a hamper. Yes, you are right, a child *could* learn to do both, but if I had to choose, it would be backrubs all the time.)

So there are ways to get people off your foot without generating a lot of negative criticism, since the negativity rarely solves anything in any case. Putdowns usually beget nothing but more putdowns. A family that creates a lot of sarcasm and putdowns will breed children with the same sarcastic and putdown mentality, and it will pass on into their own family life in all the years to come. What an ugly future!

It all boils down to the bad old red pencil mentality which looks for perfection in everything but ends up seeing only the imperfections, the flaws. And it does not take long for even a young child to catch on to the fact that Mom and Dad make mistakes and are less than perfect themselves. In self-defense against the criticism that gets heaped on them, children pour energy into looking for flaws in their parents, brothers and sisters.

The vicious circle is well-launched on its destructive, endless way.

CHAPTER 7

ANGER

Thinking back to the gossamer threads we visualized as linking two people in any real relationship, I mentioned that those shocks which we send down the thread are often the direct result of some disappointment the other person has given us, some sign of disapproval, something that the person at the other end of the thread has done or failed to do that we feel compelled to correct or improve.

The examples are endless: someone wears something which somehow threatens us; they either look dumpy, or too sexy, or too youthful or too middle class. How quickly we can feel the disapproval. Or the disappointment can reach monumental proportions when you go back to the hometown of a spouse and see him or her regress under the spell of being in their childhood livingroom again. Then there is the fundamental agony of disappointment and disapproval when you catch someone you love make a fool of herself or himself at a party, or do something harsh or stupid in the basic pattern of childrearing that makes you cringe and wonder, could I really love this person, a person who does *that?*

Sometimes the shocks we send down the thread are fairly mild, given almost thoughtlessly

"I honestly feel it's difficult
for love to flourish in a world
of capless toothpaste!"

out of habit. But there are many times when the shock is severe, a real lightning bolt—and is accompanied by an anger all out of proportion to the apparent cause.

Something as trivial, say, as leaving the cap off the toothpaste will set off a lightning blast: "Damn it, I wish you would manage to put the cap back on the toothpaste at least once before I die." There are lots of feelings behind such small issues. It is only toothpaste, but the offended party may be fairly choking and trembling with rage or coming close to tears.

Obviously, something more is represented by that missing toothpaste cap than meets the eye.

Thomas Gordon has given us a valuable insight into this mystery of overreactive anger. He suggests that the anger is a secondary emotion, a device which the outraged criticizer uses without thinking for several, not always clear, reasons. It may be to attract some attention to a far deeper or more serious problem which is generating pain or hurt. It might be to avoid that pain or hurt. Sometimes anger is learned in a violent society afraid of its tenderness and vulnerability.

Or the toothpaste cap, for instance, might be seen as a sort of symbol by the person who suddenly gives the enormous hot shock of negative criticism. In some way that we do not fully understand it is tied to an expression of anger which in turn rises out of a feeling of neglect. The cap represents just another (and very minor) example of the many ways in which the offending party is seen not to love and care for the offended party. Perhaps he or she is afraid that the love relationship is dying, that in a hundred ways, large and small, the loved one is saying, "See, I don't really care for you the way I once did."

These deep-seated anxieties and hurts come surging up from the subconscious and the distant past. Many other times in our earlier lives we have been hurt in similar ways. Missing toothpaste caps just arouse those early hurts and, programmed the way we are, we cannot easily admit to pain and fear and vulnerability so we shout and storm and throw things or slam doors. Anger is what we convey instead of hurt.

So the next time you feel the hot surge of anger welling up and you are getting up power to send a mean, wounding, irretrievable shock down the gossamer thread connecting you to someone you care for, stop and think for a moment. Search out the real feeling. You are experiencing anger, but underneath is a much more complicated array of emotions. Look for what it is that you really want to tell the other person. It would be far better to say, "Hey, please, I love you. I want you to pay more attention to me, show me that you care, share more of yourself with me. I love you and need you. I can't do without you."

That is certainly the opposite of negative criticism and it has nothing to do with anger. In fact, it can actually serve to validate the other

person, to set the action—the attention, care, and love—flowing back towards you. It's what you really want. Ironically, the name-calling anger only serves to send it in the other direction.

Not stopping to look for the real reason behind anger and negative criticism could mean that you are too unsure, possibly scared and baffled by the emotional problem that lurks behind it all. Because deep psychological problems and needs can be involved, it is frightening, and you cover your insecurity and fear automatically with these bursts of angry negative criticism. They are really shouts for help, but they seldom come through to the person you care for as such. Who wants to help you when you are cutting them to shreds?

If you work at it honestly and bravely, you may well discover the real problem. It may be that reading or counseling can help. But one of the keys to understanding and eliminating the swath of destruction negative criticism cuts through our lives is to learn how to look for these areas of deeply covered fragility, fear, or vulnerability, and to understand that they cause people to lash out with the knives of negative criticism and anger when what they are really feeling is hurt, fear, or pain.

CHAPTER 8

SIX FILTERS FOR NEGATIVE CRITICISM

If the swath of destruction resulting from negative criticism is as widespread as I believe it is and the damage it causes is so nearly permanent in nature, lasting for a lifetime, then we should regard it as a highly dangerous phenomenon, indeed. It should be recognized as the wild and ruinous weapon it is and it should be used as infrequently as possible, with a lot more caution than a physician prescribing valium or any other drug.

We have seen that people have every right to say, "Get off my foot!" We have seen that we live with a pervasive red pencil mentality and should fight against it. But aren't there times when it is your duty to give negative criticism? Personally, I am strongly convinced that good is rarely done, duty seldom fulfilled, by giving negative criticism. It almost never really helps the person who is its target; it does not help to improve them or make them grow.

People love to believe that their constructive criticism has helped others, but I challenge you to list six times in your life when you remember changing for the better because of

criticism you received. However, I realize that I am not going to abolish negative criticism just by stating this conviction—though I am going to continue my all-out campaign against it. If you feel compelled to criticize in some situations, would you at least consider putting it through the six steps, the six mental filters that I am going to list?

They will certainly help to cut down the amount of criticism you put out and they will make the criticism more effective and less destructive by aiming it at the real change you want to see made in the person to whom it is directed. It will really motivate people to get off your foot.

Picture yourself in a particular situation, a gossamer thread relationship with someone. You look down that thread and see something you disapprove of, something that disappoints you, something that seems to be screaming to be criticized. Now hold it just long enough to run what you are about to say through these six filters:

FIRST FILTER

Is the person in any shape to receive this criticism right now? Has he or she just come home from a hard day at the office? Has he just had a flat tire on the expressway? Is she hot, tired, run-down, drained? In spite of the fact that you have been sitting here all afternoon working yourself up to give forth with this richly deserved criticism, now is just not the time to let it fly.

And even if *you* feel that the person is in good shape and that the time is right, you had better check things out a little with a bit of mood sampling. Your own impatience to get at it cannot really be the governing factor.

SECOND FILTER

Are you willing to stick around long enough to help pick up the pieces? The norm here is, "Do I care enough about this relationship that I am really not just out to stick in the knife and leave the victim lying there bleeding in the alley? Am I just going to dump and run or do I care enough to stay with this criticism and work it through to a resolution?" Are you willing to stay up all night if that is what it would take? Nothing less will do. Because, if you are not willing to do that, then you have not earned the right to give that particular criticism.

One of my strongest reservations about the early encounter group, sensitivity training movement was that it brought a bunch of strangers together, opened everyone up, encouraged them to chop each other into tiny pieces with the knives of negative criticism and then sent them home to bind up their wounds on their own. There was really no commitment in those groups to help people, to stay with them.

It is an essential part of a good gossamer thread relationship, one that you want to keep intact, that if you send a shock of criticism down that thread, you have got to be willing to stay up all night, to come back day after day, to remain with the person you have criticized until you get the full impact it has had and work it through toward a solution.

THIRD FILTER

How many times has the person heard this criticism before? Unless you face that question and answer it honestly, you risk becoming nothing but a nag.

"Can't you ever remember to take out the garbage?"

Garbage . . . Garbage . . . Garbage! The person who hears that every day—or three times a day—and takes in the full shock the negative criticism carries, cannot help but regard the source as a tiresome nag. No one needs to be told, or really profits from being told, over and over again, that he or she is overweight, that her room is a mess, that he is too short, that her hair is a hopeless tangle, that his mouth is too big. Simply repeating a criticism does nothing to resolve the reason for making it—in fact, it may work actively in the other direction.

FOURTH FILTER

Can the person do anything about it? No one in his right mind would go up to a paraplegic in a wheelchair and say, "Why don't you get out on that floor and dance?" But there are thousands of parents who say to their children, "Don't be so shy, go out there and ask somebody to dance." Yet the young person may have a problem of shyness which renders him virtually as crippled as the person in the wheelchair.

So, the one who is doing the criticizing must ask, "Can the person I am criticizing really do anything about what I'm pointing out, given the circumstances he or she is presently in?"

The encounter group movement is strewn with wounded people who were told, "You talk too much"; or "You don't talk enough"; or "Your voice is too high-pitched—you sound as if you are squeaking instead of speaking."

Obviously, if the person with the high-pitched voice could hear the difference or was able to find the right pitch, he or she would do so. The problem is precisely that the person cannot find it or discern the difference or has a disorder of the vocal chords. But it is not something that the person is able to control, no matter how often he or she is told about it.

So you have got to be sure that the person criticized is able to do something about it. It is very difficult to be certain about this with strangers, and difficult even with persons with whom you enjoy a gossamer thread relationship. You may feel you know a person well enough to say with brash confidence, "You're darn right he could do something about that if he really wanted to." But this is not necessarily true. There are complicated factors behind people's resistance to change. There may be serious limitations hidden away where you cannot see them. People are made in complex and mysterious ways and the psychiatrist who

"Is this filtered criticism?"

knows all about all of them has not yet
been born.

FIFTH FILTER

Are you positive that none of your own
hang-ups, your own deep-seated psychological
needs, hurts or fears, are causing you to
make this criticism?

We talked about this in Chapter 7, but if
somehow your potential criticism has made it
through the first four filters, this one may well
cut it off at the pass.

Ask yourself, "Am I so wholesome, so pure in
motive, that I am giving out with this criticism
solely for the benefit of the person I am directing
it to?"

"Am I positive that my genuine concern for
this person is really at the heart of this criticism,
or is it possible that something in me has been
threatened or triggered? Is it possible that this
criticism represents my need to punish or
squelch or perhaps get even with this person?"

Recently, in a speech, I made a Freudian slip.
I wanted to say the words, "constructive
criticism." But it came out "constrictive
crudicism." I think I was more accurate in
my slip.

But, if you are really positive that your motives
are shiny clean and pure as the driven snow,
then pass on to . . .

SIXTH FILTER

Are you sure that what this person needs
is another criticism; wouldn't they be better

off or better motivated to change by some appreciation or validation instead?

This final filter asks you to weigh the benefits of criticism against those of affirmation. Isn't it possible, even likely, that your target will come to a better sense of his or her own worth and a better perception of self-esteem if acclaimed for good qualities instead of being criticized for something you see bad or wrong?

When self-esteem is built up by acclamation, it begins to create a self-image strong enough to do its own confident evaluation. The very thing you feel justified in criticizing may well be perceived by a person who likes what he sees about most of his behavior and who is self-motivated to make the self-correction. Could we ever hope to teach our children a more valuable set of skills?

It is true that this final filter slows things down and requires you to play the waiting game—to take a chance. But if you do not hold back the criticism and substitute the acclamation you will never know, will you, whether the person will self-correct?

That's why it is the final filter; it should serve to cut off virtually all negative criticism.

Which, and I make no bones about it, is what I'm after. Not eliminating "Get off my foot" but filtering out the vast numbers of red pencil corrections, "constructive" criticisms, and putdowns which threaten all of our gossamer thread relationships.

CHAPTER **9**

MAMIE PORTER'S THREE QUESTIONS

But, you ask, what if it is the very nature of your job to train and supervise people? It would seem to be impossible to do such a job effectively without resorting to criticism.

There certainly are such jobs or roles. In many ways it is the job that nature and society assign to all parents. It is built into the teacher-student relationship. It would seem to be inherent in the jobs of supervisors, foremen or forewomen, office managers, and others. In fact, sooner or later, to varying degrees, most people find themselves cast at least temporarily in such a supervisory-training role.

The question is a very important one: How can you make it clear to those you are supposed to be training or teaching when they are doing what is good and right and when they are doing something wrong or bad?

I would like to answer the question by telling you about Mamie Porter. She is a woman of vast talents. She supervises student teachers at Austin College, Texas. Her job is to sit in the back of the room while young teachers confront their first "live" classes. She is to evaluate their efforts, give them feedback on the class, tell them what they did right and wrong.

If you have ever been supervised, you know the feeling the presence of the supervisor generates in you.

Mamie's is a difficult and sensitive assignment because the young student teachers are usually scared stiff at the prospect of having their efforts judged right on the spot. Teaching is a profession which understandably has broad guidelines and criteria to begin with. By which I mean that it is difficult to say categorically that, on the basis of a few minutes of observation, that a person is a bad teacher or a good one. In fact, teaching may be more of an art than a science.

Mamie has three questions which she puts to the student teacher after each session. When the pupils have left the classroom, she goes up and sits down beside the student teacher.

First, she asks the new teacher to think for a moment and then discuss in as much detail as she (or he) can, *"What did you like about what you did?"*

Mamie's assumption, based on long experience, is that there is at least a little of the artist in everyone and that all artists have a capacity for self-perception and self-correction. And so the student teacher usually comes out with a fairly objective account of what she did that was right and fitting and true to the art of teaching. It is not a bragging trip, but it does affirm the things the young teacher felt she did well.

". . . and what did you like about class today?"

Mamie's second question is this: *"If you could teach the class over again, what would you do differently—what would you have changed, and how?"*

This is like giving an artist a chance to change or retouch a canvas, or letting a writer do another draft of a manuscript. Anyone who is performing a complex task should have the opportunity to look at what has been done, evaluate it, and consider what might have enhanced or enriched it.

You will note that Mamie has not uttered a single critical word so far. Yet perceptions of what was right and what was wrong about the job at hand are making themselves evident. Mamie works on the very sound theory that the only things the student teachers are really going to be able to change for the better are the things that they recognize as needing to be changed, and that they feel, at some level, *able* to change.

It's not that Mamie hasn't observed things that could be done better or that she would do differently. But then that would have been how Mamie would have done them, and not the way the young teacher would or could do them. Mamie knows that the students who are learning—who really want to do their best—will uncover most of the things that they have been doing wrong provided they are given the security of knowing that they are not going to be frozen by a stab of paralyzing negative criticism. All the beginning teacher's creative and self-correcting faculties have been left free to

77

help with growing. These same faculties may even turn up a problem that the student perceives to exist but does not know how to deal with—yet.

Which is exactly the point at which Mamie asks her third and final question: *"What help do you need from me?"*

I think that Mamie Porter is a remarkably open, wise, and sensitive woman—and very good at her job. We can all learn a lot from her. Can you imagine, for instance, the rich parent-child relationship that could begin to grow if parents applied Mamie's three questions imaginatively and consistently to all sorts of situations?

Suppose, for example, that a child is being taken to visit his grandmother. The child gets restless and cranky and behaves in a way that upsets both parents and grandmother. Instead of simply yelling, "The next time we go to grandmother's I want you to behave— you made everyone upset and miserable the way you carried on," why not sit down with the child and ask: "What did you like about going to grandmother's house? If we go again, what would you do that's different? What can your father and I do to make your time at grandmother's more fun for you?"

You might be amazed at the sort of response you get from the child. Perhaps only something negative from the first question, or just indifference to the second. But in response to the third question the child might say, "Well, it's a long, long drive there and back and I think about that and get tired. I would be better, next time, if you would remind me to go to bed a lot earlier the night before."

The child is on to the problem now; his self-correcting faculties can go to work without the freezing stab of negative criticism. The next visit to grandmother's is very likely to be a much happier time for all.

I received a very personal demonstration of just how amazingly effective Mamie Porter's three questions can be not long ago at a workshop I was conducting.

We had just completed a session devoted to explaining and applying these same questions. One of the participants was a woman who was very aggressive in her questioning. After each of the previous sessions she had come up to me and made a lot of criticisms about how the workshop was going. I didn't like it very much, because I don't like aggressive behavior *or* being criticized. It was just before the evening session and I was hurrying along a path between two buildings, planning on the way. But this woman was hot on my tail. She caught up with me and said, "I would like to raise a few issues about that last session."

"Look," I said, "I'm very busy and I'm going to be late for tonight's session, and I won't make everyone wait on your account."

My voice was harsh; I simply turned on my heel in the gravel path and walked away, feeling very pleased with myself for escaping so quickly. But almost at once I realized that I had not solved anything, that she would catch up with me later. And she did, around noon the next day.

She came up to me and said, very gently: "What did you like about the way you treated me yesterday evening on the path?"

I had to smile. She had gotten to me, softened me up.

"The only thing I liked about it was that I felt I had maintained my integrity about not being late to the session," I told her.

"The next time—this time—what will you do differently?" she asked.

"This time I will have the courage to say that I am frightened by you."

"Anything else?"

"Yes, I probably should have realized that you simply want to get the most out of the workshop—that you want to grow and learn."

"Well, then," she asked, "what help do you need from me?"

"I need your forgiveness and time to sit down and talk to you," I told her.

She gave in and we did sit down and talk. She came down off her critical high horse, and I became less threatened, and we got on a whole lot better, thanks to Mamie Porter.

CHAPTER 10

HOW TO HANDLE NEGATIVE CRITICISM

To put it as plainly and forcefully as possible, the way to handle negative criticism is simply not to tolerate it. Don't stand still in the alley waiting for those knives to cut you to pieces. Don't get caught in the confining destructive pit of the honesty trap that wants to make you think that negative criticism is good for you.

Confronted with someone who is slashing at you with negative criticism, learn to give off the message loud and clear: *"Stop! I don't need this, I don't want it, and I won't accept it. I don't grow from that."*

I think it would be marvelous if some mechanical genius could actually make a device which incorporated the six filters described in Chapter 8 that could be attached to the mouths of those who go about spouting negative criticism without thinking—a nice, compact, but highly effective little device. No matter how nasty the criticism going in, if it passed through all the six filters, nothing negative would come out.

Unfortunately we are not likely to find such a genius or get such a wonderful little black box. So, the next best thing for the person on the receiving end of negative criticism to do is to install an imaginary black box in their ears to do the filtering right there.

Don't accept anything except what finally emerges from the filter—and that should not be negative. Don't take it to heart. Don't run to meet the knife.

The point is not to "buy" any and every negative criticism that comes your way. And it will come, because most people do not know how to apply the filters to *their* mouths.

Keep that firmly in mind as a sort of ultimate defense mechanism, because I know and you know that criticism is savage and quick and fully capable of coming at us so fast that it is often impossible to get those defense mechanisms up in time, to abstract ourselves cooly from the situation and apply those six mental filters.

Negative criticism can sneak in and hurt you almost before you know what's happening. But that's no reason to let it sink into your vital areas, no reason to let it twist the knife and leave a permanent wound to fester and hurt you the rest of your life.

And the way to fight it is to immediately fall back on that ultimate defense weapon and say, "Hey, that doesn't pass through the filters. I'm not going to accept it. I don't need that." And then you should get to work healing, counteracting, neutralizing any wound you may have gotten in the quick attack.

The best way to do this is simply to start validating yourself. Through self-appreciation you immediately begin to replace any chunks burned or cut away from your self-esteem. In our other analogy, it is the way you smash the vulture eggs before they get a chance to hatch and pursue you.

Let's say you are a high school teacher and a student pops into the classroom suddenly and says: "This is a lousy class. It's boring and I'm not getting anything out of it. It's your fault. You don't teach—you just make things seem more complicated."

OK, that hurts. It came out of nowhere, fast and nasty.

But you know automatically that it is not going to pass through even the first two filters, much less all six of them. But call to mind—to write them down is much better—all the things you know you have been doing right in the class. Remind yourself of past successes, of good things that other students have said about you and the class. Think of all your students who have graduated with honors and who have burned up the track at college, or whatever else you like to see of your work show up in their lives. Tell yourself that you have a far better idea of how effective a teacher you are—your own faults and shortcomings, even—than this person who has just whizzed in out of nowhere to dump on you and run.

And think about why the person did it. Just to hurt you? It cannot be because he thought it would improve you or improve his chances for a better grade. It is more likely by far that this angry, hostile outburst is a cover for some other emotion he is experiencing—fear of failure, worry about his ability to concentrate and move along at the same speed as the rest of the class, a reaction to some criticism that he has taken to heart long ago, or something else from his vast past. All of these are possible and one of them is highly probable. He simply converted his fear or hurt or distress into anger which somehow drove him to dump on you.

Considered in this light, the criticism, this strange attack, bears no more relation to reality or a real reflection on you than some imaginary encounter with a creature from outer space.

That is the way to handle negative criticism: reject it, don't accept it, and then mop it up, neutralize, sterilize, kill it, heal it, stomp it to nothing with counteraffirmations and self-appreciation.

It is not cowardly to avoid criticism. It is not cowardly to be innoculated against smallpox. Both are a kind of preventive medicine. In the next chapters, we'll look at the other ways in which you can live a life freer of that red pencil mentality.

CHAPTER 11

A NEW THANKSGIVING

"I don't want to go home for Thanksgiving," one of my students told the class one evening. "As soon as I walk through the door my father is going to say, 'Your hair needs cutting . . . How come you're wearing those faded dungarees again? . . . Did you work off that incomplete in English? . . . When was the last time you polished those shoes?'"

"I mean," she went on, "he won't even wait till my suitcase hits the floor before he starts to dump on me. The whole vacation would simply go on and on with a string of criticisms like that."

Others in the class said they experienced the same thing when they went home for the holidays. Yet, what can you do?—home is where you go, there is no place else.

So we decided to brainstorm the problem. "What can we do about this destructive, painful situation?" And finally someone came up with an idea—an approach. The student who had started the discussion said she would be willing to put the theory to the test, change her mind and go home for Thanksgiving.

When she returned after the holiday, she gave us her report.

Sure enough, as soon as she walked in the door her father started in with his nonstop criticisms. But she did stop him—physically. She went up close to him, cupped his face in her hands and said, "Daddy, I am home. I really don't need your criticism right now. What I need is your love."

He started to cry; she started to cry. They sat down and had one of the most meaningful talks of their entire lives together. He told her—admitted to her—that he was anxious about her happiness, her success, her well-being. But he now realized that the only way he had found of expressing these things was through harping and carping at her—leaving everything else unsaid.

She tried to explain how this came across to her, and that there were other ways he could show her his love and concern. She also agreed that there were some things she was quite willing to change if they were making him so anxious—because they were little things she could change quite easily.

The approach was tested and, for one student at least, proved highly effective, clearing up a destructive and painful situation that she could not endure—and yet found impossible to avoid.

In effect, she said, "Stop, I don't need this continuous criticism—I won't accept it, and it's getting us nothing but hostility and pain." But she used gentleness and love in her approach to the one criticizing her.

LOVE IS
NOT HAVING
TO ENDURE
CONTINUOUS
CRITICISM

Wouldn't it be wonderful if all growing children could somehow be equipped with such an idea—such skills—for clearing up the fog of the red pencil mentality, to stop the attacks of negative criticism before they cut a permanent swath of destruction between you and the people you love?

CHAPTER 12

VALIDATION BUILDS STEEL CABLE RELATIONSHIPS

At the end of Chapter 3 it was noted that some people have managed to armor, strengthen, and develop the gossamer thread of their relationships with those they love or care about to the point where the bonds become more like super-strong steel cables than fragile threads. One of the big points of this book is to try and discover how those unusual people accomplish this.

The secret to good relationships—steel cable relationships—within the family and with friendships that last and last and last, is first to know all the things we have discussed about the destructive swath of negative criticism, all the things to do and not to do when dealing with criticism in all its insidious forms. The second part of the secret is to armor-coat your gossamer thread relationships with validations, affirmations, and appreciations.

Where such steel cable relationships exist, you can be sure that you are dealing with families and friends who have learned to use the word "honesty" in its full sense, so that it is not limited to the negative end of the scale, but

The Steel Cable Relationship

includes honest affirmations of love—head-thrown-back, no-holds-barred appreciations, validations not hidden away but sent out boldly and frequently, nourishing the other person's continuing delight.

In such relationships, perpetually strengthened and built up by validations, there is too much affection, too much respect—almost a reverence—to leave room for negative criticism.

Just go visit or have dinner with such people to see how quickly this is confirmed. They don't put each other down; they don't carp and pick. They listen to each other's stories without interrupting; they laugh with each other, not *at* each other. Their humor is a mutual enjoyment of the other's richness and wit. In dozens of ways, large and small, they show how much they both appreciate and then work to enhance the other's worth—the other's self-esteem—their mutual esteem.

Are such people, those possessed of steel cable relationships, somehow so perfect as to be unreal? How can two people exist so in harmony with each other? Is it a gift borne down to special people by angels?

Of course not. People in such relationships have their moments of difficulty, their disappointments, their disagreements, their mutual hurts and fears just like everyone else. But they have built up such a "backlog" of affirmations and deep respect and such a history of working these difficulties out without inflicting the knives of criticism on each other that they can usually get right through the inevitable "get-off-my-foot" issues cleanly and quickly. Those incidents which can sever more fragile gossamer threads with thoughtless name-calling and endless shocks sent up and down the thread, make only reparable dents in the carefully forged steel cable relationship.

When you get the chance to relax with certain validating families, you can almost see that network of steel cables glistening from one person to another. These are families where people are known to be trying their best, but where there is also a tacit permission to fail without having to pay a penalty for the next twenty years. There is kindness and gentleness, but there is also a lot of laughter and banter over each other's human foibles. There is a recognition that each of us is different and that there is no law that says everyone has to act, respond, and think like everyone else. There is room for that uniqueness to come alive. Without criticism, people are seen as charming, funny, different. There is also almost no red pencil mentality at work in such families.

In a family plagued and saturated by the red pencil mentality, on the other hand, there is an artificial norm into which everyone is expected to fit. There is a tenseness as everyone watches for the least deviation from this artificial norm of perfection—artificial because it is a fantasy which in fact does not exist in any one person—

or in reality. Here there are unlimited opportunities for criticism and shocks are being sent around the family room so that one feels that if the lights were turned out it would look like a battle scene from *Star Wars*.

Now, obviously, you don't build steel cable relationships overnight. I said that they are forged from consistent and long-term validation patterns.

So let's be absolutely certain what is meant by validation. First of all, though it may sound and even seem like it, validation is not praise as such. In my definition, praise is what you give when you have an ulterior motive (even if it is a good one). Praise implies that you want to produce some behavior modification. Praise is used as a sort of bribe, a handful of verbal M & Ms. Its relative is flattery, usually delivered so that the person who receives it will think more kindly about the person doing the flattering. Sometimes we just want them to give in on some point. Any way you say it, praise is controlling.

But validations are a genuine, motiveless, recognition of another in a creative, loving, and admiring way. They are a spontaneous feeling of respect, reverence, love for the other's beauty and/or spirit of life.

A real validation must not only be *thought,* it must be communicated to the other if it is to begin building those steel cable relationships. For example, a parent may go into a child's room at night. Everything is fine, but the child

"Is this praise or validation?"

moves slightly so that the covers slip away. The parent readjusts the blanket and in doing so is struck by the child's beauty. An overwhelming feeling of the child's preciousness wells up in the parent. The pride he or she takes in just seeing the child there suggests the warmest and most affirming sense of just how perfect and right the child is for that parent. That could be validation in one of its purest forms.

It is unfortunate, however, that when morning comes, that sense of warmth and love and appreciation is forgotten. Too often it is washed away in a stream of red pencil criticisms: "Did you remember to brush your teeth? Why are you rubbing your eyes all the time? Go comb your hair."

The validations have been lost—certainly to the child.

Wouldn't it be marvelous if instead of carping, the parent said to the child: "Hi! Good morning! Did you sleep well? I went into your room last night and you sure looked like you were an angel and you still do."

And, if it is absolutely necessary, because of the rich balance a nice validation provides, a parent could still add . . . "If you haven't already done so, why don't you run and brush your teeth and wash your face while I get your cereal and toast ready."

Now that is just a tiny validation on a quiet morning, but it is the start of something big— something loving, lasting, and infinitely valuable to forging the sort of steel cable relationship that will gradually become stronger and stronger. It comes with a lifetime guarantee; no knife of negative criticism can ever cut through and sever it.

A LAST WORD

This book is a sincere effort to look freshly at something which many, many people take for granted—that when you find something negative about somebody, you damn well better tell him or her about it. Most of the current thinking in the human potential movement uses a lot of energy focusing on abundant and careful rules for giving feedback, but has yet to face the problem that perhaps negative criticism should not be given at all.

Part of your understanding of this book depends on whether or not you feel negative criticism is as destructive as it sounds. If indeed you are aware of that destruction, then it is incumbent upon you to begin to practice and teach others the techniques and methods of validation, encouragement, and appreciation.

We can no longer tolerate the pervasive spread of the lack of positive self-concepts in our society. We can no longer condone the vast numbers of people bleeding from the knife wounds of negative self-criticism. If the red pencil mentality is as rampant as I believe it is, then we must find ways in both families and schools to stop its wasteful process.

In the remaining pages of this book I have provided almost two dozen specific exercises to work on the problem of negative criticism. Many of the exercises are creative ways to get validation going in your life and in those around you. They should be extremely useful for parents, teachers, and group leaders.

For me the hope is clear—a world in which people like themselves but are not narcissistic, a world full of people who can both love others and allow themselves to be loved because they feel worthy enough to accept love. Judging from the groups in which I have applied these practices, people can regain their gentleness and tenderness, and have that deep reverence for life which clearly defines the kind of people we were meant to be. For we are all capable of building love relationships free of negative criticism and the destruction it engenders.

Validation Exercises

The following exercises have been grouped into categories based on use (to be used alone, in family groups, etc.), but there is no particular order in which they are to be done. Simply pick those that seem to fit your situation and inclination.

Group I
SELF-VALIDATIONS

Exercise 1
A Validating List

Make a quick list of ten to twenty things you genuinely like about yourself. Post the list where you can see it. The refrigerator door or bathroom mirror are good spots. The list will serve to remind you of what a good person you really are. You might also code them. Mark each item with the number of months or years you have believed it to be true of yourself. Make a special mark on those items which were most recently affirmed in some way. Mark those items which you definitely would like to have recognized by another person.

Exercise 2
Validations You Would Like to Hear from Others

Take a piece of paper and divide it into four sections. Write the name of someone important to you at the top of each section. Then under each name list the validations, affirmations, and encouragements you would like that person to say to you more often. You can code these items according to how often you would like to hear them and date them according to when you heard them last. Check the items you feel you could ask the person to do for you. Finally, you might ask yourself what you could do to encourage this kind of validation from the person in question. Teachers could well use

Self-Inventory

these exercises with their classes, remembering, however, that they should always do the exercises on themselves first.

Exercise 3
When Others Put You Down

If you are a self-putdowner, how do you handle yourself when others put you down? When negative criticism comes your way, do you feel you deserve it? Even if you are a person of great confidence, how do you handle negative criticism? Make excuses? Defend yourself? Or accept it as justified?

Make a list of incidents in which you were given criticism that led to an important change in your life. (Many people cannot think of even five examples. Does that tell you anything?)

As a strategy to ward off negative criticism, you can practice delivering the following get-off-my-foot messages:

"Stop, that doesn't help me grow."

"I don't need that from you."

(The next one is hard because it is so alien to what we have been trained to believe.)

"I won't listen to your criticisms. I'm well aware of what I need to change, and I'm working on it, thank you."

Or from the Jackson Browne song:

"Don't confront me with my failures, I'm aware of them."

"75% objectivity isn't too bad."

Exercise 4
The Vulture: Fighting Self-Putdowns

The vulture refers to the self-putdowns we are all too ready to make. This exercise asks you to take each of the vulture areas discussed in Chapter 5 (IQ, social, family, creativity, sexual, and physical) and list as many validations for yourself as you can for each area. You may be surprised and delighted at how long the list can grow when you take an honest, but positive, look at yourself.

Group II
VALIDATIONS IN THE FAMILY

Exercise 5
The Dinner Table

The family dinner table continues to be one of the most underutilized places in our lives for getting good things going. All it needs is a little structure.

Some mealtime take a few minutes for each person to give a validation to some designated member of the family. If it goes well, this can be done once or twice a week. Some other evening the family can deal with such validation topics as: The best validation I gave someone at school or at work today; the person I wish would validate me and what I would like to hear; someone I feel could use more validation and what I could do about it; the best validation I received this week. The variations are endless. It just takes one of us who cares to get it moving.

Exercise 6
An Inventory for Parents

Use separate sheets of paper for each child. Draw a line down the middle. On the right side write the word "Validations." On the left, the word "Criticisms." Then think of the last thirty things you said to each of your children. Record as many validations as you can remember in the right column and as many criticisms as you can remember in the left column. Don't waste time

"My husband's inventory ratio went up 60% last week."

feeling guilty if it does not come out the way you think it should. Just plan now, for tomorrow, to change the ratio.

Exercise 7
Birthday Variations

Birthdays are such important events that validations should be a vital part of the celebration. At the simplest level, just after everyone has sung *Happy Birthday,* I recommend that individuals take time to publicly say validations to the birthday person. Just wait till you see the face of someone you care for when he or she receives so many public validations.

Another way of doing this is to write down validations on little slips of paper and give them to the birthday person. Or still another is to write out validation slips for each year of the person's age and hide them around the house in places where the birthday person would be likely to find them. Each newly found slip becomes an additional birthday greeting and validation.

Exercise 8
Husband and Wife Inventory

Use the same format as for the Parents' Inventory, but this time list the validations and criticisms you have given to your husband or wife or life partner in the past week. See what the ratio is, and plan to improve it in the weeks to come.

Group III
VALIDATION OF FRIENDS

Exercise 9
Birthday Validations

This works for friends, of course, as well as for family members. See the suggestions under the family grouping.

Exercise 10
Validation Envelopes

At the personal growth workshops I conduct, we always have a whole wall of personally decorated envelopes with each participant's name. Throughout the week people write and deposit dozens of validations in these envelopes. A rule of thumb is that for every one you receive, you write two. And does it ever mushroom! People seem to really cherish the validations they receive (and I assume, the ones they write) and many people carry them with them to read when life gets them a little down. The validations can be displayed for you to see regularly. One person I know did a collage of hers and put it up on the wall by the entrance of her home.

Exercise 11
Notes and Telegrams

Writing on blank Western Union telegram forms can be a special occasion for validating. Blank forms are available from W.U. A simple note of special validation is certainly welcome

"I know that this validation
will mean more than any present
could . . . HAPPY BIRTHDAY!"

by the person being validated. Notes of appreciation for things that people do for us are ways of validating that have almost been forgotten in this society.

Exercise 12
Telephone Validation

This might be the time to telephone a friend. It might be such a surprise that the call itself creates validation that has not occurred for that person in months. Ma Bell may be money grabbing, but she is generous if you stay under one minute. We urge people to make one-minute long distance phone calls. They can begin by saying: "I have some things I have to say to you" . . . and give as many validations as you can in one minute, ending with (if you wish) "I love you." Then write a letter and tell them all the news in your life. You may start a chain reaction of telephone calls, for which Ma Bell will be grateful.

Exercise 13
Validation Forms

With the miracle of paper reproduction, we can do all kinds of things loaded with validation potential. We can have little forms printed up and begin to slip them into our correspondence, put them under people's breakfast plates, drop them into lunch bags, etc.

Forms that say:

You are lovable and capable because . . .

I've been thinking of you with love
because . . .
I want to validate you especially . . .
I've noticed something wonderful about
you . . .
It's so easy to see good things in you.
Here's one . . .
Mother and Dad love you . . .
I love you because . . .
You make everyone around you happy
because you . . .

Exercise 14
The Unsent Letter

This strategy and the next one are from the fertile mind of Janice Koskey, a brilliant teacher and friend of mine from Lynne, Massachusetts.

Ms. Koskey would sit down and write a letter she knew she would never send. Of course, it vented a lot of feelings in a way that never hurt the other party. It also gave her a chance to look at the issues more clearly, so that when she did sit down with the so-called offending party, an enormous amount of rationality emerged since no one was being hurt. The hurt was all in the unsent letter.

Exercise 15
My Perfect Fantasy

Here Ms. Koskey invented an ingenious way of conveying some feelings that could be seen as negative but which were lifted beyond that point by her thorough examination of the issues via this strategy. There are three parts to it, and each person in the conflict must do all three.

First, describe as nonblamefully as possible what you yourself would do in your perfect "fantasy handling" of the situation between the two of you. Then describe how the other would be in the perfect handling of the same situation. Finally, tell how both of you together would be in dealing with the troublesome situation.

Exercise 16
Validation via Cassette Tapes
For important people in your life who live some distance away, a very meaningful way to deliver validations to them is through your voice on a cassette. In some ways, it has even more power than if you write them.

Group IV
THINGS TO DO WITH A GROUP OF FRIENDS

Exercise 17
Negative Criticism Skits
One of the most exciting strategies we have ever done involves grouping three to five people and giving them about ten minutes to put together skits showing some realistic examples of negativity running rampant in a family, in a group of friends, or in a love relationship. They are often grim skits, sometimes hilarious, and show the absurdity of the red pencil mentality. There is something uncannily universal about the skits, too. The processing which follows rams home some needed changes in our lives if we are to eliminate destructive criticisms.

Exercise 18
Strength Bombardment
This is an old but useful strategy. One person gets put into the center of the group or in a focus seat and everyone else in the room tells that person honest but good things that they like, respect, appreciate or admire about them. Eventually everyone in the group gets a chance to be bombarded.

Exercise 19
Validation Laboratory
Let everyone in the group agree to conduct an experiment. For five days, let them concentrate

on giving validations to one or two people, different people—a person who works in the cafeteria; the custodian; a person who works the check-out in the supermarket; the bus driver; etc. But for the period of five days all of the group agree to give a validation each time they see that person. They have to be genuine validations—no flattery or praise, just careful efforts to look for something new, fresh, and beautiful about that person and take the time to *say* it. At the end of five days get together to talk about the results.

Exercise 20
Daisy, Rainbow, and Kite Validations

There are graphic ways of getting groups to do validations. Give each friend a piece of paper with a drawing of a daisy with many petals. Then have them go about the room and ask each person to write a validation on each of your petals.

The rainbow validations work by having everyone color a rainbow and put a pot of gold at the end of it. The pot of gold is filled with validations which people collect from other friends in the group.

The kite graphic shows a kite flying and its tail becoming a series of validations. The longer the tail, the longer the validation string, hence, the higher the kite flies.

Exercise 21
Surrogate Validation

A partner is chosen and the two people talk a

little about the important people in their lives. Then, each partner picks one such person to represent and tells the other partner who he or she is. What follows is two minutes of validations to the surrogate as if they were the real person in your life sitting in front of you. The partner then gives two minutes of surrogate validations to a person in *their* life whom you are representing. It gets easier if done several times.

When this is done by each partner, they talk about whether or not they would be able to do this to the actual person. If so, when? At different times, additional precious persons in our lives can be validated in surrogate form.

Exercise 22
Validations of Difficult People

An important exercise is to identify people in your life who are difficult to validate. For many of my students, it is often one of their parents. Many of us get into that pattern of seeing everything wrong about some people in our lives. This exercise, again in surrogate form, asks if you can, for two minutes, overlook the imperfections, dissatisfactions and disappointments and give that difficult person two minutes of straight, honest, validation. It is a real challenge and an important tool for combatting the red pencil mentality.

Before closing, I wish to acknowledge the enormous debt of gratitude I owe to Harvey Jackins, the creator of Re-Evaluation Counseling. It is from Jackins that I first learned the power of Validation and its importance in creating a safe environment for working on our lives. So many of these strategies have grown out of my understanding of Jackins' ideas. He and the people in the Re-Evaluation Counseling movement deserve my fullest thanks.

Learning Magazine

Dr. Sidney B. Simon conducts weekend workshops in touching and/or values clarification in many major cities in the country. If you would like to receive an announcement and be put on the mailing list, please send a self-addressed, stamped #10 envelope to:

Dr. Sidney B. Simon
Box 846
Leverett, Mass. 01054